Original title:
Christmas Sparkles and Midnight Snow

Copyright © 2024 Creative Arts Management OÜ
All rights reserved.

Author: Wyatt Kensington
ISBN HARDBACK: 978-9916-90-888-4
ISBN PAPERBACK: 978-9916-90-889-1

Gleaming Memories in the Silent Dark

The tree was trimmed with odd-shaped baubles,
A cat sits proud, pretending it's noble.
Tinsel glows while cookies burn,
Who knew that baking could take such a turn?

Laughter bounces off the walls,
As Uncle Joe tries on the Christmas shawls.
A dance-off starts, who's got the moves?
With every twirl, the joy just grooves!

Magical Hues of the Snowy Twilight

The snowflakes fall like feathers' glide,
Kids outside on the giant slide.
Hot cocoa spills on someone's shoe,
It might just be the best one, too!

A snowman shrinks, his buttons flee,
While someone claims he's winking at me.
With frosty breath, we sing off-key,
Yet even that is pure esprit!

Glitters of Wonder on Frozen Ground

The lights strung high on every tree,
Twinkling like a wild jubilee.
Grandma's sweater, three sizes too big,
She wobbles in, doing a jig!

Snowball fights erupt with cheer,
But dodging dads brings a crunchy fear.
Sleds crash hard, oh what a sight,
The laughter echoes into the night!

Serenity Wrapped in a Silver Veil

The night is calm, but the mood is wild,
Mom's lit up like a child re-styled.
She grabs the wrong drink, but we don't care,
"Here's to the festive joy we share!"

A chorus rises, the carols clash,
As Uncle Bob tries to light up the stash.
With sparkly hats and cheer so bright,
We dance like fools in delight tonight!

Illuminated Journeys Through the Snow

As I trudge through the fluff,
I trip over my own feet,
A snowball takes aim well,
And lands snug on my seat.

The trees are dressed in white,
Like grandmas at a dance,
I laugh at their stiff moves,
But it's too late for a chance.

Sleds zoom with joyful kids,
Whipping past like a flash,
I pull my trusty board out,
Watch out for that big crash!

With a hot cup by the fire,
I'm plotting my next stunt,
But when I slip on my mug,
Turns out my move was blunt.

The Gentle Glow of Winter Mornings

The sun peeks through the clouds,
Like a cat with a sly grin,
I'm ready for adventures,
Just as the fun begins.

The snowflakes dance like pros,
Beware the naughty ones,
They swirl right into my nose,
And vanish—so much fun!

Little critters scurry wide,
Hiding treats from the cold,
I think I heard a snowman,
Whispering secrets bold.

With laughter in the air,
And a cheerful hot brew,
We'll march through winter's dance,
And make mischief anew.

Silvered Dreams and Frosty Delights

I woke up to a scene,
So bright it hurt my eyes,
The yard's a snowy kingdom,
Where only silliness lies.

As I shoveled the steps,
I found glitter in the frost,
Did Santa drop his bling?
Or have I gone and lost?

The cats are on a mission,
To conquer the white hills,
But they slip and they slide,
With all their funny spills.

My cheeks are red from joy,
And I can't feel my toes,
But laughter fills the air,
As winter's spirit glows.

Beneath the Shimmering Solstice

The lights are all aglow,
As winter's chill unfolds,
I dance like a warm pizza,
In layers thick as gold.

The stars are cheeky sparks,
Twinkling just for me,
I trip over the dog's tail,
While he laughs, oh so free!

The bench awaits my weight,
But it's made of ice blocks,
I plop down with a thud,
And now I'm stuck in socks.

Hot cocoa in my hand,
I smile at this delight,
For life's a funny journey,
With laughter as our light.

Silvered Shadows and Glowing Paths

In the night, the lights twinkle bright,
A squirrel does a dance, what a sight!
He spins and he twirls, with such flair,
 Chasing shadows, without a care.

With snowflakes landing upon his nose,
He hiccups and sneezes, then promptly froze.
A snowman nearby starts to chuckle and grin,
As a rogue snowball flies, oh where to begin!

The trees stand watch, all frosted in white,
While elves behind them plot mischief tonight.
With giggles and laughter, they scatter around,
Building a snow fort, defending their ground.

Beneath the moon's glow, the world is aglow,
While snowmen plot battles we'll never know.
In a snowy showdown of whimsy and cheer,
 The joy of the season feels perfectly near!

Whispers of Joy in a Crisp Midnight Air

The night wears a blanket of crisp, cool delight,
As whispers of mischief dance under moonlight.
A cat in a coat prances, prouder than most,
While the neighbors all gather to share in a toast.

A hot cocoa cup spills, oh, how they all laugh,
While snowflakes drift down like a cheeky scarf.
The dog jumps in snow like a foolish young pup,
And the crowd lets out giggles when he lands right up!

With cocoa and cookies, the feast starts to grow,
As children take turns in the freshly laid snow.
They craft tiny forts with all of their might,
And wait for the snowball fight to ignite!

But wait! What is that? A raccoon in a hat!
Sneaks past the reindeer, where's he got at?
The midnight air dances with joy everywhere,
As laughter and kindness fill up the cold air!

Frosty Ballets of Shimmering Light

A snowflake flutters, an elegant guest,
Spreading out wings at the final behest.
It twirls with delight, a frosty ballet,
While wise owls chuckle from trees far away.

A mouse in a scarf tries to join in the fun,
Leaping and sliding, oh what has begun!
But down he goes, into a snow bank so deep,
With giggles resounding, he'll never lose sleep.

The quaint little village, with rooftops aglow,
Hosts dancers of winter, all putting on show.
With jigs and with spins, they dance 'neath the moon,
While frost creeps around like a friendly raccoon.

So come join the merry, no need for a dress,
Just hop in the snow, it's a seasonal mess!
The air filled with laughter, returns with a shout,
While everyone joins in, for fun's what it's about!

Twilight Glows in Nature's Silence

At twilight, the snow makes everything gleam,
While critters emerge to plot mischief supreme.
A hedgehog with sprigs on his back prances free,
In a wintertime waltz, oh how lively is he!

The trees softly creak, with no hint of a sound,
As snowflakes tap dance upon frosty ground.
A bear with a bow tie hums a soft tune,
While his friends all look on, some giggles in bloom.

In nature's stillness, the laughter crescendos,
A snowball takes flight, goodwill it bestows.
The world wears a blanket, pure white and serene,
Yet the fun of the season bursts like a dream.

With lights all a-twinkling, the starry night glows,
And even the moon plays peek-a-boo, who knows?
So gather together, let merriness flow,
In the hush of the twilight, let laughter bestow!

Nurtured by the Light of Winter's Blanket

Under layers of fluffy frost,
Snowmen dream of a snack not lost.
With carrots slipping, wobbly eyes,
They giggle gently beneath the skies.

Cats in sweaters prance with glee,
Chasing snowflakes like wild bumblebees.
While dogs in boots look quite absurd,
Leaping for cakes that aren't even stirred.

Hot cocoa spills like a winter spree,
As mugs tip over on top of the tree.
Marshmallows float, dancing about,
While sugar dust sprinkles a joyous shout.

Frolicking with lights that twinkle and gleam,
Even the snow men join in the dream.
With ornaments flying, what a big mess,
We laugh till we cry, for joy we confess.

The Dance of Light on Icy Streets

Twinkling lights on roads so slick,
Watch out for that ill-placed brick!
Kids skating, graceful like a swan,
Then right on their backs, they're suddenly drawn!

Dancers in coats that are oversized,
With mittens that clash, oh what a surprise!
They twirl and stumble, trying to skate,
While grandmas chuckle—'A bit late, mate!'

Icicles hang like a Christmas choir,
Singing notes that are slightly dire.
With each sharp edge and every twist,
Who knew winter fun could be such a tryst?

Sleds zoom past in a rush of joy,
As laughter echoes from every girl and boy.
The streetlights pop like an awkward show,
Illuminating giggles in the snow!

Shimmering Echoes of a Frostbitten Dream

A frosty breeze sings a silly song,
As snowflakes twirl and start to get strong.
They tickle noses, then swirl around,
With cold, frosty kisses that dance on the ground.

Penguins in hats strut with pride,
While snowball fights happen on every side.
With laughter ringing through the ice,
Each hit's a giggle, oh isn't that nice?

Flurries swirl like confetti in air,
Who needs the beach? We're happy up there!
The cookie dough's missing, the milk's gone dry,
Did Santa's reindeer munch it as they flew by?

Beneath the stars, we freeze and we shake,
With warm fuzzy socks for our chilly sake.
What fun it is, this playful delight,
As visions of snowmen dance far into night!

When the Frost Paints the World in White

The world sparkles under a glittery spell,
But the cat thinks the snow is a personal hell.
He jumps and he leaps, then lands on his tail,
The snowman laughs, it's a comical fail!

Buddy tried to build a strong fort,
But ended up gluing an elf to his snort.
With icicles dangling like jester's caps,
The whole scene's a circus, with all of its laps!

The whole family dons their best get-up,
Waddling outside like a snowy cup.
Mom's lost her boot, Dad's slipped and fell,
As they grapple for giggles, they all yell, "Oh well!"

In this white wonderland, we tumble and roll,
Each frost-kissed moment brings joy to our soul.
With smiles and chuckles, our hearts are aglow,
In a world that's all white, we find room to grow!

The Enchantment of a Winter's Glow

Flakes fall down like fluffy bees,
They tickle noses, chill the knees.
A snowman winks with a carrot grin,
Where did his scarf and hat begin?

Sleds zoom past, oh what a sight,
One face plants, and what a fright!
Laughter echoes through the air,
As winter weirdness pulls us bare.

Hot cocoa spills on fuzzy socks,
A sweet adventure with silly clocks.
The world is dressed in white and cheer,
But so are we, with sticky smear!

We chase the lights, like sparked up flies,
Under the glow of winter skies.
With jingle bells and giddy glee,
Let's dance around a frosty tree!

Crystalline Visions of Tranquility

The ground is crisp, like crunchy fries,
Every step elicits squeaky sighs.
Jackets zip up, and hats too tight,
A snowball fight ignites the night.

Carrots in snowmen's noses twitch,
Like winter's joke, a perfect pitch.
Snowflakes land on tongues so quick,
We laugh but feel the chilly trick.

Sliding on ice, we dance, we glide,
Trying to find our balance, wide-eyed.
A tumble here, a fumble there,
Hot cider spills — oh sweet despair!

Yet through the mischief, joy will ring,
Winter's magic makes our hearts sing.
With frosted breath and silly fun,
A season's spell has just begun!

Velvet Nights and Starry Dreams

The frosty air, a chill so nice,
We join the sledding, who'll play dice?
Around the tree, we twist and chat,
Oops, I lost my Christmas hat!

Midnight's laughter hangs so bright,
As we wrap up in twinkling light.
Elves in snow, we jest and play,
Making snow angels in disarray.

A mug of cheer, we grasp so tight,
Did I just add salt? Oh, what a fright!
With marshmallows floating in the brew,
At least the laughter's still brand new!

Each snowflake whispers tales of fun,
As we chase the moon, oh beware the stun.
In this joyful bliss, we find our glow,
The chilly winds, they come and go!

The Secret Language of Frost

Whispers of winter tickle the night,
As socks and mittens have a snowball fight.
'Twas just a pebble — not a clump!
But watch your step on that frosty hump!

Giggling kids in a flurry dance,
Caught in a spin, oh what a chance.
A rogue snowball flies from the side,
Oops! Hit the neighbor — let's go hide!

The stars above, they seem to giggle,
As we fumble through, just like a wiggle.
Snowflakes chuckle, they fall with jest,
In this wacky place, we're truly blessed!

So let the ice wrap us in cheer,
With every snowdrift, let's draw near.
A winter tale of silliness unfolds,
In the frosty charm, our laughter molds!

Enchanted Shadows of the Season

In the dark, a squirrel sneezed,
Snowflakes fell, and all was teased.
A snowman grinned with carrot nose,
While a penguin slipped and fell, oh woes!

Jingle bells on tiny feet,
Running fast, oh what a feat!
The cat got stuck in tinsel bright,
A twinkling mess on a frosty night.

Sideways sleigh rides down the lane,
Driving grandpa absolutely insane.
The cookies vanished, who would know?
The pups must have put on a show!

Mittens dancing in the breeze,
Giggling kids, they just won't freeze.
Under the moon, the laughter soars,
The season's magic, who could ignore?

Beneath a Blanket of Shimmering White

Underneath a snowy pile,
A sleeping cat with dream-filled smile.
He sneezes once, then twice, oh dear,
Snowflakes flutter down like cheer.

The snowballs start as friendly play,
But soon turn into a fray!
With laughter loud and giggles bright,
Each throw's a hit, what a sight!

A snowflake landed on my nose,
Then melted fast, oh how it goes!
I tried to build the biggest hill,
But rolled away, what a thrill!

The snowman's hat, a floppy thing,
Tipped to one side as he starts to sing.
The flags of jollity all unfold,
In laughing warmth against the cold.

Midnight Glows and Winter's Embrace

The moonlight glints off frosty paws,
As rabbits play and take their pauses.
With twinkling stars up in the sky,
A winter dance, oh my, oh my!

The carolers with frozen tongues,
Forgot the words, all out of lung.
The icy gifts from Santa's sleigh,
Left laughter echoing through the day.

Jack Frost racing round the trees,
Making ice art with the greatest ease.
But tripped on a toy left out to greet,
Now he's swirling on his frosty feet!

With cocoa spills and marshmallows bright,
We toast to all through the chilly night.
A goofy grin, a wink, a cheer,
Making memories, year after year.

Lighted Paths in the Stillness

Along the path where chandeliers glow,
A dog in boots begins to show.
He jumps in piles, makes quite a scene,
With sparkles of snowflakes, oh so keen!

A penguin waddles in a line,
Wearing mittens, looking divine.
With each step, he slips and slides,
A funny sight as he collides!

The lights above flicker with glee,
While kids sneak gifts like bumblebees.
They giggle loud, and oh so bright,
In the soft glow of a winter's night.

The bells ring out, so crisp and clear,
With jingles that whisper, "Cheer, my dear!"
Each dance and step makes hearts expand,
In the joyful night, hand in hand!

Frosty Kisses on Quiet Streets

Beneath the twinkling stars, we slide,
In slippery socks, we take a ride.
The snowflakes tickle, oh what a sight,
Laughing together in the frosty night.

Neighbors peep out with cups in hand,
Wondering if snowmen are part of the plan.
With carrot noses and hats made of fluff,
They laugh at our attempts, say, "That's enough!".

We chase each other, slipping with glee,
Barely dodging a snowball aimed at me.
The laughter echoes, as snowmen fall,
Who knew winter fun could be such a ball?

So here's to the nights that sparkle and gleam,
With frosty kisses that make us beam.
In the shivers and giggles, let joy abound,
On these quiet streets where fun can be found!

Radiance in the Twilight Hour

As twilight falls, the lights reveal,
Illuminated snowflakes that dance and squeal.
We pull on our boots, ready for play,
Laughing as we tumble in a silly ballet.

A snowball fight breaks, out of control,
Snowflakes flying like tiny, fluffy souls.
We dive and dodge, all in good cheer,
With red noses shining, never a fear.

The twinkling glow of street lamps glow,
As pajamas peek out from beneath the snow.
With hot cocoa in hand, we can't stop, oh no!
Making snow angels, we're all in the flow.

In these moments of silly delight,
We dance with the stars in the chilly night.
May the joy linger long, through winter's embrace,
Radiance found in this fun, frozen space!

Celestial Lights in Snowy Veils

With scarves wrapped tight, we step outside,
In a world of wonder, we once again glide.
The snow transforms us into playful sights,
As we laugh and jostle in snowy delights.

Snowflakes twirl, as we make our way,
Building goofy shapes, let's call them play.
A friendly competition, who builds the best?
The prize is a smile, and a well-earned rest.

The moon peeks down, a wink on the game,
Lighting the chaos like fire, not tame.
With each little giggle, our cheeks rosy bright,
In this flurry of fun, everything feels right.

So come join the joy, let's dance in the freeze,
With warm hearts and laughter, we do as we please.
In the icy wonderland, we take our stance,
Under celestial lights, we can't help but prance!

The Magic of Frosted Yesterdays

When memories frolic in each snowflake's throng,
We reminisce about silly things that went wrong.
With snow angels made and mittens that stray,
We laugh at the slips, in this icy array.

Our cheeks are flushed, our spirits collide,
As we weave through the snow like a clumsy slide.
The magic abounds in our familial fun,
As we recall tales of old winter runs.

Misplaced snowmen and lost warm hats,
Digging up treasures—like forgotten cats.
With every rough tumble, we find a new way,
To celebrate life in its frosted display.

So let's raise a mug to the chilly delight,
To laughter and joy that spark in the night.
In the frosted echoes of years gone past,
We find that the humor in life is a blast!

Glittering Flurries Upon the Ground

Tiny flakes twirl in the night,
Falling down without a fright.
Snowmen frown with coal for eyes,
Waving hats beneath the skies.

Sleds are flying, laughter so loud,
Fido's buried, quite proud.
Losing mittens on the run,
Who needs fingers when it's fun?

Hot cocoa spills on my last sleeve,
I should know better, I can't believe!
Marshmallows float like fluffy dreams,
Sipping slow, or so it seems.

Quirky antics in winter's chill,
Jumping and slipping, what a thrill!
Snowball fights with laughter's punch,
But that snow never braced for lunch!

Celestial Whispers on the Breeze

Stars twinkle with a cheeky grin,
As snowflakes spin and dance in spin.
Lively folks with scarves so bright,
Trip on ice, oh what a sight!

Cookies burn, another bake gone wrong,
Dancing in the kitchen, singing a song.
Pet cats slipping from chair to floor,
Paws sliding, oh the feline roar!

Up on rooftops, the critters creep,
One returns, the other's asleep.
Rooftop games with sleighs and cheer,
Oh, no! Here comes my nosy deer!

Chasing laughter down snowy lanes,
Snowball fights with friendly gains.
A snowman hat made of a pot,
What a fashion statement, why not?

Midnight Magic in a Crystal World

Frosty panes with playful wit,
Dance around, don't dare to quit.
Hiccups from hot cider in hand,
Who knew laughing could be so grand?

Mirrors of ice where squirrels zoom,
Gathering acorns inside the room.
Tinsel tangled in a cat's tail,
A festive chase, oh what a trail!

Chilly noses and rosy cheeks,
Riding reindeer—'neigh' all the freaks!
Having fun like there's no tomorrow,
But sliding home brings a bit of sorrow.

Dreams of snowflakes crafted anew,
As silly snowmen start to stew.
With carrot noses starting to melt,
Is that laughter or just the cold's belt?

The Quiet Dance of Winter's Light

Under glitter from above,
Gifts are tucked with clumsy love.
Wrapping paper fights begin,
As dog pounces on the kin.

Sleds and bobs on frosty hills,
Squeaky boots and joyful thrills.
Pine trees dressed in blinky tat,
Who knew they could wear that hat?

Snowflakes whisper secrets low,
As children giggle, the wild winds blow.
Yet one dear soul forgot their shoes,
Slipping about with snowy blues!

Good times ring like bells so bright,
In this season, all feel light.
Laughter wraps us like a scarf,
Join the fun, hear winter's laugh!

The Soft Chill of Night's Embrace

A snowman slipped, said, "Oh dear!"
Fell right down, forgot his rear!
The owls hoot in laughter so bright,
As snowflakes dance in the moonlight.

The icicles hang, sharp as a knife,
Beware, my friend, don't live your life!
A squirrel dressed up, a fashion show,
Fluffy tails in the gentle glow.

Hot cocoa splashes, a creamy cheer,
The marshmallows swim, wave, and appear.
Laughter erupts as the snowflakes fall,
'Tis the funniest season of all!

Under the stars, we laugh and play,
With snowball fights that last all day.
Cold noses, warm hearts, we're all aglow,
In this chilly embrace, joy we sow.

Hushed Melodies of Winter's Arrival

A penguin slips on ice so slick,
Waddles around, oh what a trick!
The trees wear coats, all frosty and nice,
While squirrels barter, a nutty price.

Bundled up, we jump and cheer,
A snowball battle is drawing near!
With each throw, laughter fills the air,
Who knew snow could lead to such flair?

The lanterns flicker, glow in delight,
Guiding us home through the frosty night.
A rabbit hops in a tiny race,
With cheeks so round, oh, what a face!

The snowflakes swirl in a wild dance,
Inviting all to join in this chance.
With smiles wide and spirits so high,
We'll toast to snowflakes that float through the sky!

Nightfall's Luster on a Frozen Landscape

The moon casts shadows, dancing tall,
While penguins slide, oh my, they sprawl!
The frostbite nips at fingers, oh dear,
Yet we giggle, never fear!

An elf lost his shoe, what a sight,
He hops on one foot, just out of spite.
The trees chuckle, branches on bend,
As laughter echoes and friendships mend.

With every twinkle, the night unfolds,
We share silly tales, each one retold.
There's magic here, in whispers low,
And snowflakes sparkle, putting on a show.

Hot cider's spilled, a toasted cheer,
Laughter erupts, full of good cheer.
In this luster, we find our glow,
In every flake, a tale we bestow.

Reflections in a Crystal Stillness

A cat in a hat with jingle bells,
Wanders through snow, casting spells.
He catches a glimpse, then pounces with glee,
On a snowman's nose that's now his, you see!

With every snowflake, the whispers grow,
The prankster fox is putting on a show.
A twisty path leads to winter's fun,
As all join in, kicking up the run!

The frozen pond calls out for play,
Ice skating mischief leads us astray.
With each joyful slip, a giggle erupts,
Winter's laughter, in snowdrifts, it clumps!

As sleepy heads rest on pillows bright,
Dreams of shenanigans dance in the night.
With warmth in our hearts, we know it's true,
That fun in the snow is meant for you!

Twinkling Stars on a Silent Night

In the stillness, lights so bright,
A squirrel slides, oh what a sight!
Frosty air, with giggles near,
A snowman winks, with lots of cheer.

Pine trees dress in glittered sheen,
A cat leaps high, its face quite mean!
Snowflakes dance, like little spies,
Whispers of joy beneath the skies.

Mittens lost in fluffy mounds,
A raccoon sneaks, with playful sounds.
Hot cocoa spills, a marshmallow dive,
Laughter echoes, we're all alive!

In moonlit nights, mischief's afoot,
Furry friends in winter's suit.
With jolly hearts and jesters' play,
We'll dance and prance till break of day.

Dreams Wrapped in Silver

In cozy corners, dreams take flight,
Woolly socks that fit just right.
Mice plot mischief beneath the chair,
While grandma snores without a care.

Snowflakes tickle on the nose,
A puppy sniffs the air, then goes!
Under blankets, stories bloom,
'Til someone bumps the gift-wrapped broom.

Silly hats on everyone's head,
A toddler rolls right out of bed!
Furry friends join in the fun,
As laughter twirls, the night's still young!

Stars above begin to wink,
We toast with drinks that spill and clink.
Under blankets, snug and warm,
We share giggles, creating charm.

Glimmering Echoes of Winter

A pink-nosed reindeer dashes quick,
To herd the snowflakes, what a trick!
Gentle winds whisper funny tales,
Of penguins on their winter trails.

Snowmen argue about their hats,
One claims it's shaped like a cat!
In frozen frames of pure delight,
Sledding races through the night.

Nibble cookies, crumbs will fly,
A couch-built fortress, oh my, oh my!
Frostbite giggles as friends collide,
In winter's wonder, we cannot hide.

A snowball fight breaks out in glee,
While grandma serves hot eggs and tea.
A warm embrace in twilight hue,
In frosty fun, we will renew!

Tinsel Dreams Under Moonlight

In the yard, a penguin dance,
While snowmen spin in merry prance.
Frosted windows, secrets keep,
A cuddly bear, fast asleep.

Wrapping paper flies around,
Amidst the giggles and the sound.
Cookies vanish in a blink,
A taste of frosting, what a stink!

The cat will pounce on shiny strings,
In feathery clouds, that birdie sings.
Rooftops sparkle with fairy beams,
While everyone's lost in sweet dreams.

Under stars that blink and gleam,
We share our laughs, each little scheme.
As snowflakes twirl, our joy ignites,
In this night of magic delights.

A Tapestry of Glittering Frost

Jingle bells ring, but not on my toes,
Caught in a snowball, oh how it goes!
A frosty mishap, my nose turns bright pink,
I trip on a flake, and down I sink!

The trees wear their gowns, all shimmering white,
While I dance around, looking quite a sight.
My hat flies away, like a bird on the run,
Laughing all the way, oh what silly fun!

The snowmen are giggling, holding their breath,
I'm turning in circles, a whirlpool of heft.
With each snowy tumble, I gleefully shout,
"Who needs a sleigh? I'll wiggle about!"

Now, in this cold wonder, I find my delight,
With frosty adventures, all day and all night.
So come join the laughter, unwind from the rush,
As we roll down the hill in a fluffy white hush!

Wreaths of Stardust in the Cold

The door's decked in garlands, all sparkly and bright,
But I've lost the last cookie - oh what a plight!
The stockings are hung, but they hide all my snacks,
I'll trade all the goodies for a few brisk attacks!

I sprint through the yard, where the icicles gleam,
While plotting revenge, with a mischievous scheme.
The neighbors all laugh, as I slip on some ice,
Who knew winter fun came with this much spice?

Giggling elves peek from behind every tree,
Trying to figure out who tripped me with glee.
With wreaths made of laughter and snowballs for cheer,
I'll take on the world, with a grin from ear to ear!

So gather around when the cold winds do blow,
Let's spin through the twilight, all covered in snow.
In this frosty kingdom, where giggles reside,
We'll make merry mayhem, come let's take a ride!

Secrets of the Frost-Kissed Twilight

Underneath the moonlight, a secret I find,
Sledding down hills is a frosty rewind!
The whispers of snowflakes dance in the night,
As I slip on a patch, oh what a fun sight!

The cocoa is brewing, but spills on my shoe,
I giggle and gasp, as my laughter rings true.
The trees start to chuckle, or maybe it's me,
In this frozen wonderland, oh what glee!

My dreams take the form of a snowball parade,
With frosty confetti, we're all unafraid.
The flurries are swirling, embracing the jest,
As we tumble and tumble, we give winter our best!

So here's to the secrets, all wrapped up in frost,
With laughter and joy, there's never a cost.
In this silly spectacle, let giggles ignite,
As we dance in the moonlight, all day and all night!

Glistening Paths Where Dreams Reside

Snowflakes are twinkling, like stars in the sky,
While I'm busy dodging a snowball nearby.
With laughter erupting from peaks and from hills,
We're crafting our memories and sharing our thrills!

The snowmen conspire with mischievous grins,
As I trip over sleds and tumble again.
With paths made of giggles and dreams in the air,
We'll journey together, no worries or care!

Frothy hot chocolate skips past my cheek,
With each joyful stumble, I'm feeling quite weak.
But who needs warm socks when the fun never ends?
Let's build frosty castles with all of our friends!

So stomp through the drifts, let your laughter collide,
In the paths where we wander, let joy be our guide.
For in this winter wonderland, wild and alive,
We'll sparkle and shimmer, oh what fun to thrive!

Secrets Hidden in the Snowfall

The flakes come down, so soft and white,
I built a snowman, what a sight!
His carrot nose is quite the feat,
But alas, he tripped on his own feet.

I laughed so hard, I lost my hat,
It flew away—imagine that!
A squirrel scooped it up with glee,
Now he wears it, too, you see.

Inside the house, hot cocoa brews,
With marshmallows shaped like little shoes.
But every sip, a giggle's near,
I spilled it once, it disappeared!

At night we dance, a snowball fight,
Snowmen cheering, what a delight!
Giggles echo through the chill,
Winter brings us joy and thrill!

Echoes of Laughter on Crisp Air

The sun peeks out, the world aglow,
Kids are building forts, on with the show!
Sliding down hills with squeals of cheer,
While penguins slide, oh dear, oh dear!

A snowflakes' kiss upon my nose,
I spin around, in winter clothes.
Yet trips abound, oh what a fall,
I laugh so hard, I can't stand tall.

The sleds race down, oh what a sight,
Tumbling down, bringing pure delight.
Who knew the snow could bring such glee?
As laughter floats like a melody.

We toss a snowball, aimless flight,
Missed my friend, and hit a kite!
The way it flaps brings on more smiles,
Let's keep this fun going for miles!

A Dance of Icicles and Starlit Skies

Icicles hang like teeth from a grin,
I swear they giggle for a win!
Underneath the stars, bright and bold,
I've tripped on my scarf, the tales retold.

Snowflakes twirl like dancers in line,
Every little whirl feels divine.
Yet one misguided flap, oh dear,
I came down soft, with a snowy sphere.

A penguin waddles by with flair,
Cracking jokes without a care.
He asks me, "What's cold and neat?"
I shrug, he says, "An icy treat!"

So we raise our mugs, a toast to fun,
With laughter echoing, we've just begun.
Around the fire, stories blend,
Winter magic, my frosty friend!

Glistening Pines and Frosty Wishes

The pines stand tall, dressed in white,
Looking like they're ready to take flight.
A squirrel slips down, what a fuss,
He's scurrying fast, he'll miss the bus!

With twinkling lights all aglow,
They blink and wink, putting on a show.
As we prance and laugh through the night,
Trip on branches—oh what a sight!

Hot chocolate spills, we share the mess,
But giggles rise, more than a guess.
The snowman smiles with a funny face,
He knows it's time for our silly race.

The frost brings chills, but hearts are warm,
With antics that can't help but charm.
So here's to laughter, and frosty dreams,
With magic sprinkled in joyful beams!

The Embrace of Winter's Magic

Frosty noses and silly hats,
Snowmen wobble, doing splits.
Sledding down the hills so steep,
We laugh and tumble, no time for sleep.

Hot cocoa with marshmallows afloat,
Elves on break, riding a goat.
As carolers sing with glee so loud,
We join in, feeling quite proud.

Under twinkling lights we prance,
Doing the snowman dance by chance.
Frost bites lightly at our toes,
But oh, the joy, it only grows!

When the night brings a chill so bold,
We chase our dreams while tales are told.
With cookies piled high on a plate,
We giggle at fate, we can't be late!

Soft Whispers of Glimmering Night

Stars are twinkling in the skies,
Brushing snowflakes with our sighs.
Pine trees wearing coats of white,
We play hide and seek in the night.

Laughter echoes through the trees,
As snowballs fly with the greatest ease.
Frosty cheeks and tangled hair,
Dance around without a care.

Chimneys puffing, smoke like dreams,
Hot pie cooling, or so it seems.
With gingerbread men making a fuss,
They laugh too, in joyous gusts!

While snowflakes swirl in shapes so grand,
We sketch our wishes in the sand.
Oh, what fun, let the antics flow,
In this land of white, we steal the show!

Enigmatic Wonders Beneath the Moon

Moonlight dances on snowflakes bright,
A raccoon dons a hat, what a sight!
With goofy grins, we skate around,
On frozen ponds, we twirl and bound.

Hats askew and scarves unwrapped,
In a snowball fight, we've happily trapped.
A plump penguin steals our snack,
We chase him off, "Hey! Come back!"

Each snowdrift holds a secret laugh,
Sleds tip over, what a gaffe!
Mittens thrown, and laughter loud,
We're the goofiest, and we're proud!

Frosty footprints on the trail,
We giggle wildly, tell a tale.
With hot fudge slipping down our chin,
The magic of winter, let the fun begin!

A Symphony of Snowflakes and Stars

A jingle jangle in the air,
A polar bear plays the tambourine with flair.
Snowflakes waltz, all aglow,
As we sing loud, "Oh, where did they go?"

Sipping cider by the firelight,
Grandpa's stories bring pure delight.
A chorus of giggles brought by the sparks,
We dance around, leaving joyful marks.

With pies and cookies stacked in a tower,
Cats in costumes steal the hour.
Wandless wizards with sugar wands,
Summon snowballs with clever bonds!

In this night of dreams and fun,
We twirl until the night is done.
So raise a cheer for laughter shared,
In the whimsical season, none are spared!

Stars Weaving Dreams in Winter Air

Twinkling lights in a frosty scene,
Frogs in scarves, oh what a dream!
Snowmen gossip, sipping hot tea,
Guess who's the best? Not me, not me!

Elves on rooftops, sliding down,
Chasing their hats all over town.
Reindeer play tag, with a jump and a hop,
But where's the sleigh? Oh, who let it drop?

Wishes on stars that say, 'Don't you dare!'
Another snowball flies through the air!
Noses all red, frozen with cheer,
This chilly season, we all persevere!

Pine trees giggle in the moon's soft light,
While squirrels choose ornaments for the night.
"Don't touch that branch!" a raccoon will say,
As snowflakes whisper, "Let's dance and play!"

The Dance of Light on Snow-Kissed Paths

Bouncing beams on a blanket of white,
Chasing stray shadows, what a delight!
Fluffy penguins on the sidewalks slide,
Hiding their giggles, trying to glide.

Dancers of glow, twirling around,
Coffee cups clatter without a sound.
"Let's build a snowman!" the children scream,
While the plump cat naps, lost in a dream.

Hats blown away by the winter's breeze,
Kind squirrels laugh as they dance with ease.
"Catch me if you can!" the bright lights tease,
While snowflakes tumble, bold as you please.

Jingle bells ringing, not on a sleigh,
But on a tricycle, rolling away.
Snowball fights breaking out with glee,
Lights all around, is this wild party for me?

Soft Glows of Winter's Serenade

Soft bubbles of warmth in the chilly night,
Fuzzy mittens in a playful fight.
Snowflakes giggle as they zig and zag,
While squirrels sing tunes with a soft little brag.

The moon's a balloon floating way up high,
Tickling the rooftops, making them sigh.
Chimneys puffing out stories untold,
As hot cocoa bubbles from mugs, pure gold.

Lights in the windows twinkling like stars,
Filled with laughter, forgetting the scars.
Each drip of sweetness, a giggle or two,
As marshmallow clouds float in skies so blue.

Funny hats that wobble and sway,
Making the short ones shout, "Hey, look this way!"
In this winter, laughter rings near,
As warm hearts gather, spreading good cheer!

Illuminated Slumbers of the Earth

Under soft blankets, the world's tucked away,
While snoozing bears dream of a sunny day.
Lights catch the eyes of sleepy old snow,
As ducks in tuxedos put on a show.

Nighttime giggles from chubby wee mice,
Wobbling around, adding fun to the spice.
The trees all hum with a rustling tune,
As owls bring stories under the moon.

Whispers of wind play a gentle prank,
On candy canes lined up in a rank.
Socks hanging low try to catch a ride,
As dreams spin around, warm hearts open wide.

Silly snowflakes, as they tumble down,
Wrap up the earth in a fluffy white gown.
With every sparkle twinkling with fate,
This cozy sleepover, so fun, so great!

In the Embrace of Twinkling Chill

The frosty air bites at your nose,
While snowmen hold hands in funny poses.
Elves on rooftops slip and slide,
Chasing their hats up a snowy glide.

Hot cocoa spills as laughter flows,
While reindeer prance in silly rows.
A snowball fight turns into a mess,
Who knew white fluff could cause such distress?

Penguins in scarves wobble and dance,
Jumping for joy, oh what a chance!
Frosted trees twinkle, it's quite a sight,
As giggles echo through the night.

With jingles ringing and smiles so wide,
We celebrate with humor as our guide.
Under twinkling lights, we all play,
In the chilly embrace of this merry day.

Night's Blanket of Frost and Wonder

Under the stars, a blanket of white,
Snowflakes shimmer, oh what a sight!
A squirrel mistakes a chair for a throne,
While pretending to call this yard its own.

The moon grins down, like a cheeky dude,
As folks in puffy jackets feel a bit crude.
Falling over in a frosty dance,
While snowballs fly, you stand no chance!

Hot snacks are stealing all the show,
With penguins on ice, putting on a show.
Snow angels giggle, flapping their wings,
While laughter fills the air and sings.

So here's to the night, frosty and bright,
With friends gathered close, it feels just right.
Amidst the wonder, joy takes delight,
In this jolly chaos and snowy fright.

Glimmering Reflections of Timeless Tales

Stories unfold under twinkling lights,
As cats chase their tails in snowy bites.
A dog leaps high, and lands with a splat,
In a pile of snow, he looks just like that!

Chasing the kids, the snowman's in fright,
As children pelt him with all of their might.
Hot dogs dancing on a frosty stick,
As everyone giggles at the humor so quick.

With gingerbread antics, cookies on trays,
The kitchen erupts in sweet, silly ways.
Frosting is flying, what a delight,
As we decorate treats into a frosty sight.

We gather together, the warmth we ignite,
In tales made of laughter and joyful nights.
With sparkles of joy, and tales to unveil,
The glimmering laughter serves to regale.

Enchanted Frostiness of the Night

The night giggles under its icy crown,
As the moon plays hide and seek in the town.
Snowflakes tumble in a whimsical race,
Landing on noses, oh the delicate trace!

Squirrels bury treasures in fluffy white,
While neighbors throw snow in a gleeful fight.
With mittens on hands, the laughter rings,
As we twirl and spin, in circles, we fling.

Frosty the Snowman wears a bright grin,
As kids shove each other into a spin.
Twinkling lights dance in raucous delight,
Under the spell of this frosty night.

Hot cider spills as joy fills the air,
With cheeks all rosy, no time to spare.
Embracing the magic that winter brings,
In the enchanted chill, we laugh and sing.

Twinkling Dreams in Winter's Embrace

In a world of snowflakes, I trip on my feet,
Wobbling like Santa, this dance feels so sweet.
Hot cocoa in hand, marshmallows collide,
I laugh with the reindeer, who happily glide.

Mittens and scarves in colors so bright,
I sneeze near the snowman, he's startled in fright.
When icicles glisten as sharp as my jokes,
The frostbite reminds me, avoid those cold pokes.

The tree on the corner sways with delight,
I chase round the kittens, oh what a sight!
Slipping and sliding, I join in the fun,
With giggles and chuckles, oh, we're never done!

So here's to the blunders, the laughs shared at night,
In this frosty kingdom, we shine oh so bright.
With twinkling dreams and a wink from the moon,
The winter's our stage, let's break out in tune!

Silent Whispers of Frosted Nights

Snowflakes whisper secrets when all else is still,
I made a snow angel, but fumbled a spill.
With snow on my nose, I giggle with glee,
The frost says, 'Get up, there's more fun to see!'

The moon grins down, with a mischievous glow,
As I slip on my boots, trying hard not to show.
A snowball is flung, it hits brother's poor hat,
Now we're in a battle; get ready for that!

Icicles dangle, sharp like my wit,
Just watch as I wobble; I might lose my grip!
The neighbors are peeking, they cheer from their door,
As I juggle the snowballs, then tumble and roar!

So let's dance in the flakes, under skies full of cheer,
This wintertime humor makes everything clear.
In our frosted domain, we twirl and we play,
With laughter and joy, we'll turn night into day!

Luminescent Joys Beneath the Starlit Sky

Under twinkling stars, I chase after dreams,
A nutcracker slips, his dance isn't what it seems.
Carols are sung, but off-key is the tune,
The snowmen are laughing, oh what a cartoon!

A sparkly sleigh, but it's stuck in a plot,
With jingles and giggles, laughter is hot.
I trip on my feet, while trying to freeze,
But a snowman outsmarts me, 'No chance, if you please!'

The gingerbread cookies are winning the bake,
But they're sprouting more wigs than I'm willing to make.

With frosting mustaches, they dance on the plate,
I can't help but chuckle; this sweetness is great!

So let's twirl in the snow, with shimmy and shake,
Each moment we share makes the cold feel less fake.
With luminescent joy and giggles that soar,
In this enchanting night, let's laugh evermore!

Frost-Kissed Elegance of the Season

Frost-kissed and fancy, I waltz through the flurries,
But trip on a snowdrift—my head swims in worries!
With snowflakes as jewels, I twirl in the night,
The squirrels all cheer, 'What a whimsical sight!'

With cocoa mustaches, we revel in fun,
In hats way too big, we all look like one.
I fashion a crown from the feathery snow,
Trendsetting my friends, we put on a show!

The cookies are missing and buttons askew,
As I slip on the ice, guess what else I do?
I land in a pile, all frozen but grinning,
The snowflakes applaud; oh, this night is beginning!

So let's laugh 'til we cry in this frosted terrain,
With snowball shenanigans—oh, what a gain!
Together we sparkle, with warmth and with cheer,
In this season of laughter, let's kick up our gear!

Celestial Glimmers on Winter's Canvas

The twinkling lights dance on the trees,
While laughter floats in the crisp night breeze.
A snowman winks with a carrot nose,
His frosty jokes make the cold wind froze.

The stars compete with the silly lights,
As pets prance around, chasing their own flights.
The sleigh bells jingle, they jolly jive,
While the cocoa spills and the marshmallows dive.

Frosty's hat is askew, oh what a sight,
Tip it a little, it's crooked tonight!
Snowflakes parade like they own the street,
While neighbors throw snowballs, a playful feat.

The snowflakes giggle as they fall from high,
Catching our noses, and tickling our eyes.
With cheeks all red, it's a winter race,
Chasing each laugh in this frosty space.

Enchanted Moments in Glittering White

In fluffy blankets, we tumble and roll,
With hot chocolate dreams in each frozen bowl.
The snowflakes whisper their frosty tales,
As we build a kingdom where laughter prevails.

The sleds zoom past with a jubilant cheer,
While yetis in pajamas bring heaps of good cheer.
Igloos sprout up like mushrooms in scores,
Filled with secrets and giggles, who knows what's in store?

With every stumble on the icy glide,
We giggle and fall, it's a wild ride!
The snow angels flap like wings in the breeze,
Messy and magical, we do it with ease.

So let's raise a toast with our mugs filled to brim,
To the silly encounters in this winter whim.
With silly hats and a bounty of jest,
In the sparkle of white, we truly feel blessed.

Chasing Shadows in the Frosty Glow

As shadows lengthen, the world glows bright,
We're dashing through drifts, what a silly sight!
The moon plays peekaboo, all giggles and grins,
As snowflakes giggle on our chilly chins.

The rabbits hop by, with a curious glance,
Who invited them here to join in the dance?
Frosty the snowman, with flair and delight,
Keeps forgetting his lines in the snowy night.

Snowball fights break out, our laughter ignites,
As we dodge and weave in our wintery tights.
With flurries around us, the night's full of cheer,
We chase down the memories, each giggle sincere.

A snow-covered bench becomes a launching pad,
For the shenanigans, oh can you believe we've had?
With each frosty sparkle, our joy multiplies,
In the glow of the night, our spirits will rise.

A Tapestry of Stars and Snowflakes

Under the quilt of the twinkling night,
A troupe of snowmen gets ready for flight.
Their carrot noses pointed, ready to play,
Telling silly stories of a frozen ballet.

With brooms for their wands, they conjure up fun,
While children whirl 'round, their laughter's begun.
The snowflakes pirouette, with a flurry of glee,
As sledding chums rocket, wild as can be.

The dog in a scarf prances off in a chase,
While we stumble in stitches, what a funny race!
Wrapped up in the joy of this frosty display,
Each tumble and giggle melts all cares away.

So gather your friends near the glittering glow,
As we toast to the tales only nighttime can show.
With marshmallow hats and a boatload of cheer,
The tapestry we weave brings the whole world near.

Dazzling Reflections on a Winter's Eve

On rooftops high, the lights do dance,
While squirrels plot their festive prance.
The snowmen giggle, a snowball fight,
As all of winter shines so bright.

A cat in boots struts down the lane,
Where snowflakes whisper, tickle, and feign.
Reindeer in front yards sip hot cocoa,
With holiday cheer, they put on a show.

Icicles hang like chandeliers grand,
While the kids make angels in frosty land.
The chill in the air laughs in delight,
As laughter and sneezes take flight at night.

So raise your mugs, let's make a toast,
To chilly fun we love the most.
With twinkling lights and snowball cheer,
We'll celebrate winter with laughter and beer.

Sparkling Secrets Beneath the Celestial Veil

Whispers of snowflakes tickle the ground,
While elves in pajamas sneak all around.
A snowman with shades raves to the beat,
While snowflakes gather for their winter treat.

The moon, so round, with a wink so sly,
Watch out for snowballs as they fly!
A dog mounts a guard, quite serious,
Yet slips on ice, looking furious.

Hot chocolate geysers erupt with joy,
As marshmallows cavort—what a ploy!
Rabbits in mittens dance on their toes,
Amidst the sprinkles and frosty prose.

As stars sparkle in the chilly expanse,
Let's throw on our boots and join the dance.
For under this veil of frosty fun,
We'll celebrate till the night is done.

The Radiance of Cold Embraces

The wind sings tunes of frosty delight,
As penguins waddle with all their might.
A snowflake tickles the tip of a nose,
Creating giggles as everyone knows.

With each frosty breath, the world's aglow,
As snowmen gossip where the cold winds flow.
Santa's reindeer take selfies with glee,
While frost-topped houses boast victory.

Little children dash with snowball plans,
While grandpa walks in comically large pants.
The lights on the trees twinkle with flair,
As snowfalls glow, filling hearts with care.

So let's pile on fun, and share a laugh,
With sledding races and hot cocoa craft.
In the chill of the night, joy sparks all around,
As stories of winter's humor abound.

Frosted Lullabies Beneath the City Lights

In the city, the lights like diamonds shine bright,
While carolers sing with all of their might.
The traffic's a snowball, all jumbled and loud,
As reindeer fly past, leading a crowd.

A cat on a skateboard zooms in the snow,
While raccoons throw snowballs, putting on a show.
The children are zooming, well bundled, they cheer,
On a sleigh made of boxes, they spread winter cheer.

Frosty the snowman dances in place,
As snowflakes pirouette with exquisite grace.
There's even a snow dog, proud as can be,
Who's chasing the snowmen—"You can't catch me!"

So gather 'round friends, let's share some delight,
Beneath all the twinkles that brighten the night.
With cookies a-plenty, and laughter galore,
These frosted lullabies we'll always adore.

Shining Magic in the Veil of Night

In the glow of silly lights,
Cats chase shadows, what a sight!
Elves in jammies, sipping tea,
Stirring up a laugh, oh me!

Snowmen say, "We're really cool!"
Waving at the kids in school.
Frosty giggles fill the air,
With squeaky boots everywhere.

Twinkling stars play peek-a-boo,
Is that a tree that's lost its shoe?
Garland tangled in the breeze,
Squirrels laughing, trying to tease.

Bells are ringing, oh what fun,
Mice are dancing, on the run!
In the night, the joy does swell,
With merry mishaps, all is well.

The Luster of Whiteness and Warmth

Pine cones toss their hats in cheer,
While snowflakes swirl, they disappear.
A cozy fire, oh what a treat,
With socks that somehow lost their feet.

Warm cocoa spills, a marshmallow fight,
Giggles echo through the night.
An icicle dangles, looking suspicious,
Watch your head—it's rather vicious!

Chasing puppies in the snow,
They dive and tumble, fast and slow.
With every leap, the fluff takes flight,
Whiskers twitching, what a sight!

Glowing windows, laughter bright,
Hats too big, oh what a sight!
In this heart of winter's charm,
No one's safe from a playful arm.

A Midnight Waltz in Shining Stillness

Under twinkling skies, we whirl,
With mischievous glee, we twirl.
Stars giggle, moon starts to slide,
As we stumble, our joy can't hide.

Snowflakes fall, each one a prank,
Matching socks are in the tank.
Dancing shadows, chasing dreams,
Belly laughs, or so it seems.

Hot tea spills, oh what a mess,
We laugh it off, nothing less.
Carrots leap right into sight,
With noses twitching, oh what's right?

Here in this waltz, we lose our way,
But laughter brightens even gray.
In the stillness, fun unfolds,
Underneath this blanket, magic untolds.

Whispers of Frosted Wishes

Whispers float on frosty air,
Mittens dry now by the chair.
A frosty hand just stole a kiss,
Oops, a blunder! Pure bliss.

Puddles glisten, icy slides,
Hot dogs join the gnome-like rides.
Giggles echo, the fun prevails,
While hot cocoa fills the pails.

Chimneys puffing clouds of cheer,
Is that laughter we can hear?
Bouncing snowballs, here we go,
Target spotted, what a show!

Under the mist, we play all night,
Gather 'round the twinkling light.
In whispers shared, our secrets glow,
Frosted wishes steal the show!

Luminescent Tales in the Quiet

In a land where snowmen dance at night,
With carrot noses and buttons so bright,
They try to ski but often fall flat,
Creating problems, oh where is the cat?

The reindeer are prancing, a clumsy crew,
Chasing their tails, who knew they could do?
They slip on the ice, with a jolly loud cheer,
Making snow angels, their giggles sincere!

In the corner a squirrel holds a snowball fight,
While a raccoon dons a hat that's too tight,
They hurl fluffy snow with glee in their eyes,
Who knew frosty fun could be such a prize?

A sleigh full of cookies goes zooming past,
With elves in the back, holding on fast,
They scatter the sweets as they whoop and they laugh,
As the village enjoys their frosty craft!

Glowing Hearths and Winter's Breath

The fireplace crackles, the marshmallows toast,
But one little ghost thinks he loves them the most,
He tries for a treat, but he's stuck in the flare,
In a gooey embrace, 'Oh dear, what a scare!'

Each stocking is filled with odd bits of fun,
Like socks that have slippers and glittery gum,
The cat finds the yarn, transforms it to art,
And unwinds the gifts while we giggle and start!

The snowflakes are falling like fluffy popcorn,
The kids hurl themselves in, their laughter is drawn,
While down the road, the old lady with flair,
Accidentally fashions a hat made of hair!

With tales of the silly, the guild of the cheer,
We dance in our boots, spread the joy far and near,
So let's raise a glass to the giggles that flow,
As the warmth of the fire keeps the laughter aglow!

Moonlit Meadows and Starry Nights

The stars shine above like a million bright eyes,
While the moon snores loudly and dreams of pies,
The rabbits come out in their fanciest coats,
Planning a party in their clever boat!

With carrots as drinks and greens as the pie,
They dance on the grass, making time fly,
But the fox in the corner just can't help but stare,
Wishing his tail was fit for a fair!

A hedgehog with glasses reads maps upside down,
As travelers giggle and run through the town,
Over puddles and snowdrifts they sing and they leap,
While the owl rolls his eyes from his perch in the deep!

When morning arrives, the laughter won't cease,
With stories of chaos and moments of peace,
So here's to the night and the silliness found,
In the meadows where whimsy and joy knows no bound!

Frosty Artistry in the Stillness

In the silence of winter, a painter takes flight,
With brushes of silver and colors so bright,
He crafts tiny snowflakes with an artistic twist,
Then laughs when his palette is suddenly missed!

The gingerbread house is a sight to behold,
Yet; the cat swipes a cookie, both brave and bold,
He climbs to the roof just to give it a taste,
And tumbles right down, what a sticky-faced waste!

The snowball brigade marches forth through the square,
But the snowman shimmies and flings a quick flair,
As the townsfolk react with surprise and delight,
Their shouts and their laughter echo through the night!

So let's toast to the joy found in each frosty scene,
With warm hearts and laughter, we're ever so keen,
For life in the chill is a whimsical show,
Where fun never fades, and the good times all glow!

Frosted Trails in the Moonlight

In twinkling boots, we stroll in glee,
A ghostly squirrel darts up a tree.
Snowflakes giggle, falling down,
Tickling noses in sparkling town.

A snowman's hat flies off in fright,
Chasing crows who take to flight.
With carrot noses, we do stare,
As snowballs whizz through frosty air.

Giant footprints lead us on,
To find where all the laughter's gone.
We slip and slide, what a sight!
Rolling down till it feels just right.

The moon winks down on our parade,
While marshmallow snowmen start to fade.
With cocoa smiles and candy canes,
We dance in circles, no refrains.

Gentle Rides on Silent Frost

We hop on sleds like birds in flight,
With joyful shouts, hearts feeling light.
Puppies tumble, making a mess,
While we try to avoid all the stress.

A cocoa stand? Oh, what a treat!
But falling snow makes standing hard to beat.
With hats askew and mittens lost,
We find delight, no matter the cost.

The chill brings laughter, jokes that soar,
While we search for hot drinks at the door.
Chattering teeth, what a little game!
Who knew winter could feel so insane?

We glide on ice, pretending to skate,
A few little tumbles don't seal our fate.
With sparkly tales and frosted fun,
In this silly world, we've already won!

Luminous Stories in the Night's Embrace

Beneath bright stars, we gather 'round,
With fuzzy socks, we stomp the ground.
The tales are wild, the laughter shrill,
As frostbite tickles, and time stands still.

Our snowflakes twirl like ballerinas,
While squirrels steal all of our zucchinis.
Ghosts of winter dance overhead,
Demanding snacks be properly fed.

The giggles rise like flurries in air,
As mittens fly, and snowballs spare.
We build a fortress made of cheer,
To fend off the ice from a long, last year.

Through moonlit chaos, joy runs free,
Every snow-laden branch holds glee.
Luminous stories weave and spin,
In the raucous night, we all dive in!

Shimmering Paths of Yesteryears

With footprints deep in fields of white,
We chase down memories of delight.
The elder folks laughing loud and clear,
As snowflakes cloak them in winter cheer.

Hats from yesteryears, so big and bright,
Tumble down the hill with a comical sight.
Spirited rides on rickety sleds,
While snowmen lose their carrot heads!

In swollen jackets, we fold up neat,
Waging snowball wars on the frosty street.
With rosy cheeks, we can't control,
These jovial antics all take their toll.

And as we settle by the flame,
Our silly stories are just the same.
We raise our mugs to nights of old,
While laughter sparkles, countless and bold!

Milton Keynes UK
Ingram Content Group UK Ltd.
UKHW020046271124
451585UK00012B/1082